Neuschwanstein Castle
The Castle that Inspired Walt Disney

Jennifer Howse

www.av2books.com

AV² provides enriched content that supplements and complements this book. Weigl's AV² books strive to create inspired learning and engage young minds in a total learning experience.

Your AV² Media Enhanced books come alive with...

Audio
Listen to sections of the book read aloud.

Key Words
Study vocabulary, and complete a matching word activity.

Video
Watch informative video clips.

Quizzes
Test your knowledge.

Embedded Weblinks
Gain additional information for research.

Slide Show
View images and captions, and prepare a presentation.

Try This!
Complete activities and hands-on experiments.

... and much, much more!

Go to **www.av2books.com**, and enter this book's unique code.

BOOK CODE

J784682

AV² by Weigl brings you media enhanced books that support active learning.

Published by AV² by Weigl
350 5th Avenue, 59th Floor
New York, NY 10118
Websites: www.av2books.com www.weigl.com

Library of Congress Cataloging-in-Publication Data
Howse, Jennifer.
  Neuschwanstein Castle / Jennifer Howse.
     pages cm -- (Castles of the World)
  Includes bibliographical references and index.
  ISBN 978-1-4896-3396-5 (hard cover : alk. paper) -- ISBN 978-1-4896-3397-2 (soft cover : alk. paper) -- ISBN 978-1-4896-3398-9 (single user ebk.) -- ISBN 978-1-4896-3399-6 (multi-user ebk.)
  1. Schloss Neuschwanstein (Germany)--Juvenile literature. 2. Eclecticism in architecture--Germany--Bavaria--Juvenile literature. 3. Castles--Germany--Bavaria--Juvenile literature. 4. Ludwig II, King of Bavaria, 1845-1886--Palaces--Germany--Bavaria--Juvenile literature. I. Title.
  NA7741.N49H69 2015
  725'.17094337--dc23
                        2015001386

Printed in the United States of America in Brainerd, Minnesota
1 2 3 4 5 6 7 8 9 0 19 18 17 16 15

032015
WEP070315

Editor: Heather Kissock
Design: Mandy Christiansen

Contents

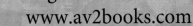

What Is Neuschwanstein Castle?

Deep in the Bavarian Alps, a fairy-tale castle rises majestically from a hilltop. Its soaring towers, steeply sloped roof, and white walls can be seen for miles (kilometers). Named Neuschwanstein Castle, it was the dream of King Ludwig II of Bavaria. He built the castle to serve as his private retreat, a place where he could escape the responsibilities of royal life.

Neuschwanstein is one of the most photographed castles in the world.

King Ludwig II built Neuschwanstein Castle in the 19th century. Inspired by the myths and legends of **medieval** Germany, the castle's design represents the **romantic** ideals of the 12th and 13th centuries. The castle also pays homage to the king's love of opera. *Neuschwanstein* means "new swan stone." The name refers to an opera called *Lohengrin* by Richard Wagner. The opera recounts the medieval legend of Lohengrin, the swan knight.

The swan is a **symbol** of King Ludwig's family.

1.4 MILLION people visit Neuschwanstein Castle each year.

Neuschwanstein Castle inspired **Walt Disney** to build Sleeping Beauty's castle in **Disneyland** in 1955.

Since taking control of the castle in 1990, the Bavarian government has spent **more than $13 million** on its upkeep.

A Step Back in Time

Neuschwanstein was one of several castles built by King Ludwig in an effort to create his own **empire**. In the early years of Ludwig's reign, Bavaria lost a war to Prussia. Ludwig lost much of his power as a result. Building castles was one way of proving his status in the country. Neuschwanstein was built near the site of Hohenschwangau Castle. Built by Ludwig's father, Maximilian II, Hohenschwangau had played an important role in Ludwig's early years. Ludwig wanted to build a similar castle to call his own. He chose a nearby hilltop that housed the ruins of two former castles. Ludwig's plan was to build a castle that was even larger, and more extravagant, than the previous two castles combined.

King Ludwig II ruled Bavaria from 1864 to 1886.

1869 Construction starts on September 5, when the **foundation** stone is laid.

1855	1860	1865	1870

1867 King Ludwig II hires **architect** Eduard Riedel to build a castle based on drawings by designer Christian Jank.

1868 Twenty-six feet (8 meters) of stone outcrop are removed to create a flat, level area on the hilltop where the castle is to be built.

1873 The Gateway Building, which serves as the main entrance to the castle, is the first part of the structure to be completed.

King Maximilian II built Hohenschwangau Castle in the 1830s. The royal family used it as their summer home.

1874 Georg von Dollmann replaces Eduard Riedel as chief architect.

1886 Julius Hofmann becomes the castle's new chief architect.

1892 The **Bower** and Square Tower are completed.

1875   1880   1890   1895

1880 The castle's **topping-out ceremony** is held, even though the building remains under construction.

1884 King Ludwig moves into the Palas, the part of the castle that houses the living quarters.

1886 King Ludwig dies at Lake Starnberg on June 13. A few weeks later, Neuschwanstein opens to the public.

Neuschwanstein Castle's Location

Neuschwanstein Castle is located in the German state of Bavaria. This region is found in the southern part of the country, bordering Austria. The castle is in a remote area, far away from most of Germany's large cities. The closest town is Füssen, which is about 3 miles (5 kilometers) west. A small village called Hohenschwangau sits at the base of Neuschwanstein. It is here that visitors can buy tickets to tour the castle.

ELEVATION On its mountaintop perch, Neuschwanstein Castle is 3,306 feet (1,008 m) above sea level.

LENGTH The castle complex measures 490 feet (149 m) at its longest point.

The castle was originally called New Hohenschwangau Castle, in honor of King Ludwig's childhood memories. It was renamed Neuschwanstein after Ludwig's death.

Its location in the middle of the Bavarian Alps provides the castle with beautiful scenery. Neuschwanstein is surrounded by rolling hills and lush forests. The castle overlooks the Pöllat **Gorge** and Lake Forggensee. The yellow towers of Hohenschwangau Castle rise up from the other side of the valley.

TOWERS Of the castle's many towers, the tallest stands 213 feet (65 m) high.

AREA The complex covers a total area of 8,500 square feet (790 square meters). The total floor space of the castle is 65,000 square feet (6,038 sq. m).

Outside the Castle

Neuschwanstein Castle was designed as a romantic version of a medieval castle. Built in the Neo-Romanesque style, the castle's features create a majestic structure.

TOWERS Neuschwanstein's towers are one of its most striking features. Soaring high above the structure, they add to the fairy-tale look of the castle. Most of the towers are round. However, a square tower rises from the Knights' House. Medieval castles were built as **fortresses**, designed to protect those living inside. Attached to Neuschwanstein's main stair tower is a **turret**. In medieval times, turrets served as lookouts. Guards stood in them to keep watch over a castle.

BALCONIES Balconies also served as lookouts in medieval times. Called hourds, they were often wooden additions to the walls or towers. Over time, they evolved into permanent structures within the castle complex. Neuschwanstein has several small balconies and one large balcony that takes up two stories. Many of the balconies offer incredible views of the surrounding countryside.

COURTYARD The courtyard forms the center of the Neuschwanstein Castle complex. From here, people can gain access to the rest of the castle. Neuschwanstein's courtyard has two levels. The lower courtyard is found just inside the Gateway Building and extends up to the Square Tower. A staircase leads to the upper, and larger, courtyard.

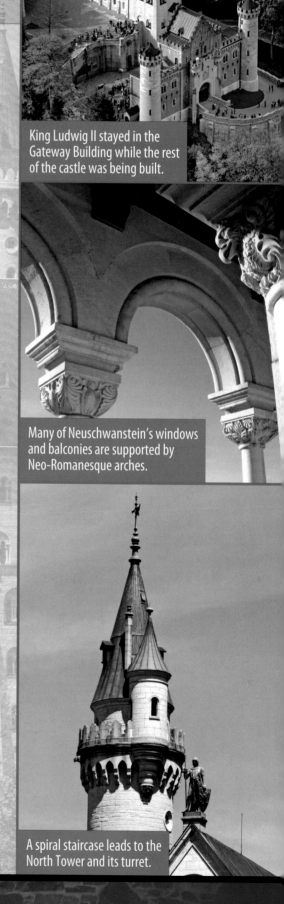

King Ludwig II stayed in the Gateway Building while the rest of the castle was being built.

Many of Neuschwanstein's windows and balconies are supported by Neo-Romanesque arches.

A spiral staircase leads to the North Tower and its turret.

The Square Tower extends to a height of 147 feet (45 m). A platform near the top of the tower served as a lookout for the castle's knights and guards.

The castle's two-story balcony extends from the Throne Hall and overlooks the Bavarian countryside.

Like other parts of the castle, the design of the courtyard was influenced by the opera *Lohengrin*.

Neuschwanstein Castle was almost named one of the **New Seven Wonders of the World**.

The Square Tower is

148 feet
(45 m) high.

Construction of the castle was supposed to take only

3 years.

2 LARGE

paintings decorate the exterior walls of the Palas.

In 2012, Neuschwanstein Castle was **featured** on the **2-euro coin**.

The upper courtyard contains markings for a **chapel** that was **never built**.

During construction, there were as many as

300

stonemasons, construction workers, and bricklayers working on the project.

Inside the Castle

King Ludwig paid great attention to creating a castle that was sumptuous in appearance. Many of the rooms in the castle are adorned with lavish works of art and elaborate decorative features.

THRONE HALL One of the grandest rooms in Neuschwanstein Castle is the Throne Hall. The room covers two floors on the east side of the Palas. Its **vaulted** ceiling has been painted blue and decorated with stars. A series of **porphyry** columns runs around the perimeter of each floor, supporting the weight of the ceiling. The floor is decorated with **mosaics** of inlaid stone tiles. A platform was created to house the king's throne, but the throne was never made.

MURALS Large **murals** cover the walls of many rooms inside the castle. Most of these murals portray scenes from Richard Wagner's operas. A mural in the king's bedroom shows a scene from the opera *Tristan und Isolde*. The salon's murals show scenes from *Lohengrin*. Other murals show chivalrous scenes of knights and squires. The Throne Hall, for instance, has a mural of Saint George slaying a dragon.

GROTTO ROOM One of Neuschwanstein's most interesting rooms has been made to look like a grotto, or cave, complete with a small lake. Artificial stalactites and stalagmites, along with artificial rocks and waterfalls, decorate the room. When the room was first built, a lighting system lit the entire grotto with different colors. This system was a new form of technology at the time.

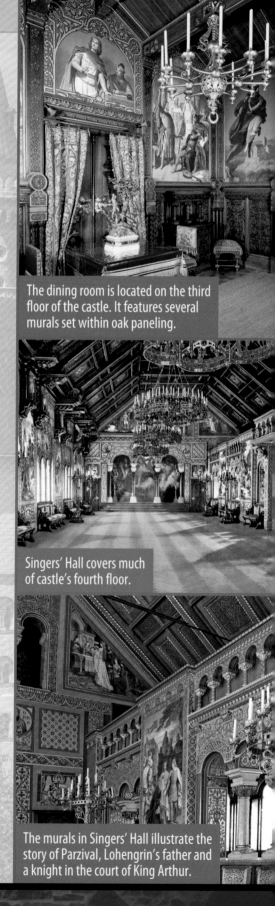

The dining room is located on the third floor of the castle. It features several murals set within oak paneling.

Singers' Hall covers much of castle's fourth floor.

The murals in Singers' Hall illustrate the story of Parzival, Lohengrin's father and a knight in the court of King Arthur.

Swans are a common motif in the rooms of the castle.

King Ludwig's bed features silk drapes that have been embroidered with patterns of lions, swans, crowns, and lilies.

The Throne Hall has been designed to resemble a church. It features an altar and religious artwork.

Out of the **200** rooms planned for the castle, only **15** were completed.

A mountain spring provides running water to **ALL FLOORS** of the castle.

The chandelier in the Throne Hall is **13 feet** (4 m) tall and weighs **2,000 pounds** (907 kilograms).

Photographs are **not allowed** to be taken inside the castle.

2.5 MILLION stone tiles were used to create the floor mosaics in the Throne Hall.

The kitchen serviced a dining room that was **THREE FLOORS ABOVE** it. An elevator was installed to transfer the food between floors.

14 workers spent **4.5 years** carving the wood in the king's bedroom.

The Castle's Builders

King Ludwig II had specific ideas regarding what the castle of his dreams should look like and the conveniences it should have. As his castle was based on literature and the arts, he initially sought help from leaders in these fields to design the building. It was only after the concept was finalized that Ludwig hired an architect to develop the construction plan. Hundreds of workers then came together to make his dream castle a reality.

Christian Jank also painted some of Neuschwanstein's interior murals.

Christian Jank Designer

Christian Jank was born in Munich, Germany, in 1833. King Ludwig commissioned him to create the conceptual drawings for the castle. Jank was a landscape painter and theater set designer. He had created several of the sets used in Richard Wagner's operas. His work on these projects attracted the attention of King Ludwig. The king asked Jank to help him with the design of Neuschwanstein and some of his other castles as well. Along with designing the exterior of Neuschwanstein, Jank also contributed to the interior design. Jank died in Munich on November 25, 1888.

Eduard Riedel Architect

Eduard Riedel was the architect responsible for adapting Jank's conceptual designs into architectural drawings. These drawings outlined the exact sizes and dimensions of all parts of the castle. Riedel was born on February 1, 1813, in the German town of Bayreuth. He began studying architecture while living in Bayreuth, but completed his schooling in Munich. He then went on to design buildings in Germany and Greece. After a brief stint teaching architecture, Riedel began working for the German government, eventually becoming the court architect under King Ludwig's father. Riedel died on August 24, 1885, in Starnberg, Germany.

As the royal court's architect, Eduard Riedel was responsible for redesigning Berg Castle for Ludwig's father.

Stonemasons use chisels and mallets to cut and chip rock into the desired shapes and patterns.

Stonemasons

The limestone **cladding** and decorative features cut into the stone walls of Neuschwanstein Castle were all created by stonemasons. These are people specially trained to cut and shape rock into a desired form and install it properly on a structure. Stonemasons must understand the **composition** of a stone block before they begin cutting it. They must also understand the grain of the stone and how to keep the stone from crumbling as they work it into the desired shape.

Wood Carvers

The interior of Neuschwanstein Castle contains many wood carvings. These carvings were created by **artisans** specifically trained to work with wood. A wood carver cuts or chisels wood until the desired figure takes shape. Working with wood requires patience and skill. Carvers can choose from a variety of hardwoods and softwoods. They have to know which type of wood will achieve the desired effect. They must also know which tools will help them create the carving. Wood carvers rely mostly on chisels, knives, and mallets to carve the wood.

Most woodcarvers have been trained in carpentry techniques.

Cement workers mix cement with sand, gravel, and crushed stone to make concrete. Concrete has been used to make buildings since ancient times.

Cement Workers

Cement was a key material in the construction of Neuschwanstein Castle. It was used to create the concrete foundation as well as to bind together the bricks that make up the castle's outer walls. Mixing cement is the key to a good foundation. A cement worker must understand how much limestone or chalk and clay or shale needs to be combined and how hot to make the mixture. The decisions made during the mixing process determine the quality and strength of the cement.

Building the Castle

The 19th century was an exciting time for advances in technology. Europe had just experienced the **Industrial Revolution**. This era had introduced new manufacturing systems and machinery. King Ludwig embraced many of these new technologies and encouraged their use in the construction of Neuschwanstein. Even though the castle was constructed to resemble a building from a previous time, it actually was one of the most modern castles to be built in the 1800s.

PICKING UP STEAM Using steam to operate machinery was one of the most innovative advances of the Industrial Revolution. Steam power helped to **automate** machinery, which made construction times much faster. Steam-powered technology played an important role in Neuschwanstein's construction. Materials could now be shipped to the region by train instead of making the entire journey by horse-drawn wagons. This greatly reduced the amount of time it took to get supplies to the area. Once the materials arrived at the construction site, steam-powered cranes were used to lift them into place. This made for a more efficient process and required less human effort than in the past.

CREATING THE FRAMEWORK While the exterior of the castle was made mainly of cement, brick, and limestone, the interior relied on steel framework to provide its strength. The builders decided to use a new method of steel construction and employed a system of T-**girders** throughout the structure. This type of girder was new to construction, and its strength was unknown. To ensure that the girders would support the weight of the building, they were made to be oversized. In the Throne Hall, T-girders were also used to support the vaulted ceiling. They were placed to form a grid pattern, with some extending across the length of the room and others across the width.

COMFORT AND CONVENIENCE It was important to King Ludwig that his castle be a home fit for a king. This meant that it had to have all the latest conveniences. Neuschwanstein did not rely on fireplaces to add warmth. Instead, the castle was outfitted with a central heating system run on electricity. Water did not have to be carried into rooms by servants because every sink and bathtub had running water. The castle even had flush toilets, which were not in wide use at the time.

In one year alone, Neuschwanstein's builders used 465 tons (422 metric tons) of marble, 400,000 bricks, and 600 tons (544 t) of cement.

Telephones, invented only in 1876, were installed on the castle's third and fourth floors.

Trains could only bring the construction materials so far. Due to the castle's remote location, horses still had to take the materials up the mountain to the construction site, much like many tourists are transported to the site today.

The use of steel in the castle allowed for the construction of large windows. This is because the steel provided the extra support needed around the openings.

Similar Castles around the World

The construction of Neuschwanstein Castle was part of an architectural trend that took place during the 19th century. Many of the castles built during this period were created as idealized replicas of medieval structures. Designers borrowed elements from various styles of architecture to create these castles. They were meant to reflect a time of fairy-tale princesses and chivalrous knights.

Alton Castle

BUILT: 1847–1852 AD
LOCATION: Alton, Staffordshire, England
DESIGN: Augustus W. Pugin
DESCRIPTION: Alton Castle was constructed on the ruins of a medieval castle that was built in about 1175 AD. The large, **Gothic**-style castle was built as a country house for the 16th Earl of Shrewsbury. Standing on the edge of a cliff, it was protected on three sides by a stone wall. Entry to the castle is through a gatehouse found at the south side of what remains of the wall. A chapel can also be found on the castle grounds. The castle's square towers, massive stone walls, and **crenellations** are all common elements of medieval architecture.

Today, Alton Castle is used as a youth retreat. Young people can stay for a day or for longer periods to focus on their personal development.

Lichtenstein Castle

BUILT: 1840–1842 AD
LOCATION: Lichtenstein, Germany
DESIGN: Carl Alexander Heideloff
DESCRIPTION: A castle has stood on the site of Lichtenstein Castle since the 1200s AD. The first castle was destroyed in 1377 during a war. The second was dismantled in the 18th century. In 1837, Count Wilhelm of Württemberg purchased the site and constructed a medieval-style castle that was inspired by the stories of the Knights of Lichtenstein, who used to live there. The castle complex has a courtyard and a thick fortress foundation that continues up to the third floor.

Lichenstein Castle's design was influenced by the book *Lichtenstein*, by Wilhelm Hauff. Hauff was well known for his fairy tales.

After years of government ownership, the 160-room Peles Castle was returned to Romania's royal family in 2007. It has operated as a museum since 1953.

Peles Castle

BUILT: 1873–1914
LOCATION: Sinaia, Romania
DESIGN: Wilhelm von Doderer, Johannes Schultz
DESCRIPTION: Built as a summer residence for King Charles I of Romania, Peles Castle was created primarily in the German **Neo-Renaissance** style. However, several medieval elements were also included to give the castle a fairy-tale look. The castle's exterior features several **terraces**, which are decorated with a variety of statues, fountains, and marble vases. The stained glass windows are one of Peles Castle's best-known features. The windows were hand-painted by more than 40 Swiss artisans. It took them three years to complete the work.

Issues Facing the Castle

Conserving older buildings can be a major challenge. The original materials used to create them can be very expensive or difficult to acquire. It is also difficult to find people with knowledge of 19th-century construction techniques. In the case of Neuschwanstein, the location itself is also at risk of deterioration.

WHAT IS THE ISSUE?

The **textiles** used to create drapes, upholstery, bedding, and banners for the castle are exposed to humidity, light, and temperature changes.

The castle was built at the peak of a small and narrow mountaintop. The mountain is **eroding** due to wind and other weather conditions.

EFFECTS

This exposure can weaken the textiles, causing them to fade or even fall apart.

The erosion is changing the shape of the mountain and destabilizing the bedrock on which the castle is built.

ACTION TAKEN

The textiles have been placed in special plexiglas® cases. These cases are equipped with technology that controls the amount of light that reaches the textiles, as well as the temperature and humidity within the case.

The areas of the mountainside that have shown signs of erosion have been covered with netting. This netting will reduce the amount of rock that falls away from the rock face, helping to stabilize the area where the castle is located.

Build a Steam Engine

Steam-powered machinery played an important role in the construction of Neuschwanstein Castle. Try this experiment to see how steam works to create energy. You will need an adult to help you with this experiment.

Materials
- Pinwheel
- Kettle that whistles
- Oven mitt
- Water

Instructions

1. Fill the kettle with water.

2. Heat the water until the kettle whistles. This means the water inside the kettle is boiling.

3. With the oven mitt on your hand, pick up the pinwheel.

4. Hold the pinwheel over the steam that is coming out of the kettle. The pinwheel should begin to turn. Why do you think this is happening?

Neuschwanstein Castle Quiz

Q Who was Neuschwanstein Castle built for?

A King Ludwig II of Bavaria

Q What is the Palas?

A The part of the castle that houses the living quarters

Q Whose operas served as the inspiration for the castle's exterior and interior design?

A Richard Wagner's

Q What was the main architectural style used in the castle's design?

A Neo-Romanesque

Key Words

architect: a person who designs buildings

artisans: workers who create products using traditional methods

automate: to convert to an automatic process

bower: a lady's private apartment in a castle

cladding: a protective layer that covers another material

composition: the way in which a mixture is made up

conserving: protecting objects from deterioration

crenellations: indented sections along the top of a wall

empire: a group of states or countries under the leadership of a single ruler

eroding: wearing away due to water, ice, or wind

fortresses: structures built to keep out invaders

foundation: the base upon which a structure is placed

girders: large beams

gorge: a deep, narrow valley

Gothic: a style of design that began in the 12th century

Industrial Revolution: a period from the 18th to the 19th centuries characterized chiefly by the replacement of hand tools with power-driven machines

medieval: relating to a period in history that extended from the 5th to the 15th centuries

mosaics: patterns or images created with small pieces of stone or glass

murals: paintings that have been applied directly to a wall

Neo-Renaissance: a design style of the 19th century that was influenced by Italian works

Neo-Romanesque: a design style of the 19th century that borrowed from early medieval architecture

porphyry: a hard rock that contains crystals

romantic: a fanciful view of what is heroic or adventurous

terraces: a series of level platforms

textiles: types of cloth or woven fabric

topping-out ceremony: an event held when a building's highest stone is placed

turret: a small tower placed on a larger tower

vaulted: arched to form a ceiling or roof

Index

Log on to www.av2books.com

AV² by Weigl brings you media enhanced books that support active learning. Go to www.av2books.com, and enter the special code found on page 2 of this book. You will gain access to enriched and enhanced content that supplements and complements this book. Content includes video, audio, weblinks, quizzes, a slide show, and activities.

AV² Online Navigation

Book Pages
AV² pages directly correspond to pages in the book.

Key Words
Study vocabulary, and complete a matching word activity.

Quizzes
Test your knowledge.

Slide Show
View images and captions, and prepare a presentation.

Audio
Listen to sections of the book read aloud.

Video
Watch informative video clips.

Embedded Weblinks
Gain additional information for research.

Try This!
Complete activities and hands-on experiments.

AV² was built to bridge the gap between print and digital. We encourage you to tell us what you like and what you want to see in the future.

Sign up to be an AV² Ambassador at www.av2books.com/ambassador.

Due to the dynamic nature of the Internet, some of the URLs and activities provided as part of AV² by Weigl may have changed or ceased to exist. AV² by Weigl accepts no responsibility for any such changes. All media enhanced books are regularly monitored to update addresses and sites in a timely manner. Contact AV² by Weigl at 1-866-649-3445 or av2books@weigl.com with any questions, comments, or feedback.